D1307053

A New True Book

THE SEARCH FOR EXTRATERRESTRIAL INTELLIGENCE

By Dennis B. Fradin

Consultant: Paul Horowitz, Ph.D.
Harvard University

CHILDRENS PRESS ®

CHICAGO

Painting shows *Voyager 2* passing Neptune and its moon Triton.

PICTURE ACKNOWLEDGMENTS

© Cameramann International Ltd.—6

EKM-Nepenthe:
© Bob Ginn—27 (left)
© Robert Eckert—cover, 27 (right), 41
© John D. Campbell—37

Historical Pictures Service—12, 44 (top left & right)

Holiday Films—5, 8 (2 photos), 9, 10, 19, 23

NASA—2, 21, 42
© Jet Propulsion Laboratory 29 (2 photos)

National Radio Astronomy Observatory—33

Gunther Schwartz—39

Wide World Photos—14 (2 photos), 31 (left), 35

Tom Dunnington—25, 44 (bottom)

John Forsberg—16, 17

Cover—Very Large Array-Radio Telescopes

Dedication: For Sidney and Diana Coleman

Library of Congress Cataloging-in-Publication Data

Fradin, Dennis B.
    The search for extraterrestrial intelligence.

    (A New true book)
    Includes index.
    Summary: Chronicles briefly scientific theories about and search for intelligent life beyond the Earth.
    1. Life on other planets—Juvenile literature.
[1. Life on other planets]   I.   Title.
QB54.F88   1987   574.999   87-14618
ISBN 0-516-01242-8

Childrens Press®, Chicago
Copyright ©1987 by Regensteiner Publishing Enterprises, Inc.
All rights reserved. Published simultaneously in Canada.
Printed in the United States of America.
1 2 3 4 5 6 7 8 9 10 R 96 95 94 93 92 91 90 89 88 87

TABLE OF CONTENTS

IS ANYONE ELSE OUT THERE?

Have you ever looked at the stars and wondered if creatures like us live on distant worlds? The universe is so vast, scientists say, that intelligent life probably exists elsewhere. But no extraterrestrial intelligent life has yet been found. "Extraterrestrial" means "beyond Earth." "Intelligent" life means creatures with

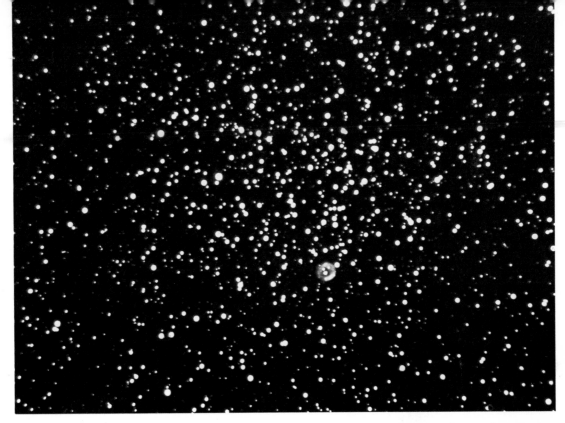

Open star cluster

good brains, like ourselves.
    Wouldn't it be exciting if
we one day contacted
extraterrestrials? They
might have three eyes,
eight arms, or other
strange (to us) features.

Astronomer records data from the radio telescope
at Kitt Peak National Observatory in Arizona.

They might be so smart
that we would seem like
bugs to them! Even as
you read this, a few
scientists are searching
the universe for signs of
extraterrestrial intelligence.

LIFE NEEDS PLANETS

The universe has many
trillions of *stars*—giant
balls of hot, glowing gas.
There are more stars than
there are grains of sand
on all Earth's beaches. But
stars are too hot to
support life.

Life can exist on
planets—objects that orbit
stars. We know that at
least one star has planets.
We call that star the Sun.
Eight of the Sun's nine

Saturn

Jupiter

planets probably have no advanced life forms. The eight are Mercury, Venus, Mars, Jupiter, Saturn, Uranus, Neptune, and Pluto. But one planet is known to have intelligent life. That planet is our lovely blue and green home, Earth.

Earth

In every way, Earth is perfect for life as we know it. Earth is neither too hot nor too cold. It has plenty of air, water, and sunlight. Thanks to these conditions, our planet is teeming with life, including human beings.

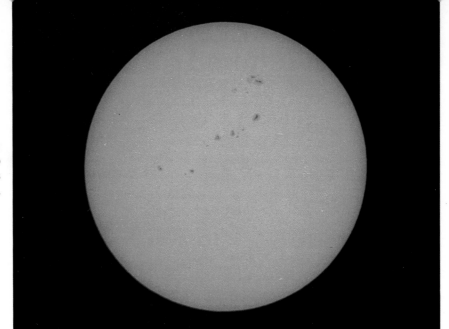

Only the Sun is known to have planets orbiting it.

Do other stars have planets that could support intelligent life? Probably, say astronomers. They know several stars have some kind of material orbiting them, but no star besides the Sun has been proven to have planets.

THREE WAYS OF FINDING EXTRATERRESTRIALS

Perhaps future telescopes will show that other stars do have planets. The finding of many planets would make it more likely that intelligent life exists out there. But it wouldn't prove it. The planets could all be lifeless.

There are only three ways to prove that advanced life exists elsewhere. The

In *From the Earth to the Moon*
Jules Verne described a moon train.

extraterrestrials could visit
us. We could visit them.
Or we could exchange
signals with them.

HAVE EXTRATERRESTRIALS VISITED EARTH?

Some people think that aliens have already visited Earth. They say that some of the unidentified flying objects (UFO's) that have been reported are alien spacecraft. A few people even claim to have gone aboard flying saucers.

Very few scientists think that any UFO's are alien

A United States Coast Guard photographer shot the picture shown above of "unidentified aerial phenomena" on July 16, 1950. A California man took the UFO picture shown below on August 3, 1965.

spacecraft. Scientists say that people have mistaken weather balloons, satellites, airplanes, and even planets for alien ships. And some people were probably simply lying.

If proof of flying saucers is found, scientists will change their minds. But no flying saucer or piece of an alien craft has ever been found. There is not even a really good photograph of a flying saucer.

VISITING THE SUN'S OTHER PLANETS

The second way to prove that extraterrestrials exist is to find them. The place to start is with our Solar System. The Sun, the nine planets and their

moons, and all other objects
that orbit the Sun make up
our Solar System.

The eight planets besides
Earth "probably" have no
advanced life. They seem
to lack the air, water, and
temperatures needed by

life as we know it. Studies made by astronomers show this. Probes sent out to the planets confirm it.

But what if a planet has a life form that does not need air, water, and moderate temperatures? This seems unlikely, but the only way to know for sure is to visit the planets.

Astronauts have already landed on the Moon. After the year 2000 they will probably start visiting the

Apollo 11 lands on the moon. Earth is in the background.

planets. Mars and Venus
will probably be first. The
other planets should come
later. These explorations
will settle the question of
advanced life in the Solar
System once and for all.

VISITING OTHER SOLAR SYSTEMS

Astronomers may soon prove that many other stars have solar systems. They may even spot Earthlike planets. People would then want to pack their bags, hop on spaceships, and visit those planets. That may not be possible. The problem is that every star beyond the Sun is so very far away.

Vast distances in space

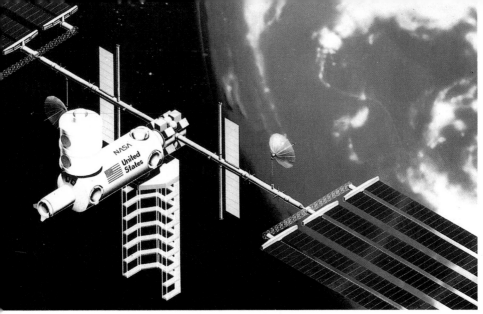

Space stations will make exploration of outer space easier in the future.

are measured not by miles, but by units called light-years. A light-year is the distance that light (which moves at 186,000 miles per second) travels in one year. A light-year is equal to about 5,880,000,000,000 (5.88 trillion) miles.

Proxima Centauri, the nearest star to the Sun, is 4.3 light-years away. In other words, going at the speed of light it would take a few years to go to Proxima Centauri and back. Farther stars would take hundreds or even thousands of years to reach traveling as fast as light.

It is a law of nature that nothing can go faster than the speed of light. This means that there is no

A spiral galaxy

way to reach a star
hundreds of light-years
away in less than
hundreds of years. There
is even worse news. We
may never build ships that
can travel 186,000 miles
per second. One that

could go that fast would
cover the distance between
the Earth and the Moon in
just over a second!

Say we build a ship that
can zoom along at a
million miles per hour.
Even at that great speed,
it would take about 3,000
years to reach Proxima
Centauri. People do not
live that long.

One day we may be
able to freeze astronauts.
They will remain frozen

(but alive) during the long
journey to a distant solar
system. Once there, they
will be thawed. Imagine if
they awoke from a 10,000-
year-long trip to find that
the planets they were
visiting had no life!

THERE'S AN EASIER WAY!

There is an easier way
to hunt for extraterrestrials.
We can pick up their
radio signals, if any
signals are being sent out.
Radio signals (which are
also produced by TV)
travel at the speed of
light. They keep going
forever into space. They
can be picked up by
special instruments called
radio telescopes.

At this moment, radio

Radio telescopes in Owens Valley, California (left) and Socorro, New Mexico (right)

telescopes on a distant
planet may be picking
up radio waves we have
broadcast. Imagine that in
the year 1987 creatures
twenty light-years away
are listening to Earth's
radio signals. They would
not get the 1987 signals,

because those signals would take 20 years to reach them. Instead, they would be hearing radio waves from 1967. They could be receiving broadcasts of the 1967 World Series between the St. Louis Cardinals and the Boston Red Sox!

In 1987 a planet 49 light-years away could get our signals from the year 1938. They may be receiving the famed 1938

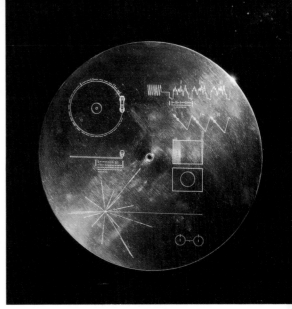

Voyager carries a record containing sounds
and pictures of Earth.

"War of the Worlds" radio
show about Martian
invaders. But in 1987
creatures 100 light-years
away would get no signals
from Earth. People did not
start sending radio signals
until eight years after the
year 1887!

EARLY SEARCHES
FOR ALIEN SIGNALS

If beings on other worlds
have developed radio and
TV, their signals could be
picked up by our radio
telescopes. The radio
signals would sound much
like static. But a radio
telescope's computers
could tell that the signals
were sent by intelligent
life. For one thing, they
would be more repetitive

Cornell University astronomer Frank Drake believes in the search for extraterrestrial life. In 1983 he said, "You get the sense that there's a lot of life out there. It will be fascinating when we learn about it."

than signals naturally sent out by stars.

A few projects have tried to capture extraterrestrial radio signals. The first one was Project Ozma, conducted in 1960 by American astronomer Dr. Frank

Drake. For 150 hours Drake hunted for alien signals with the radio telescope at the National Radio Astronomy Observatory in West Virginia. Drake captured no alien signals.

Drake and other early searchers had a big problem. They could only study one radio channel at a time. Radio waves can be sent over billions of separate channels. Listening to just the

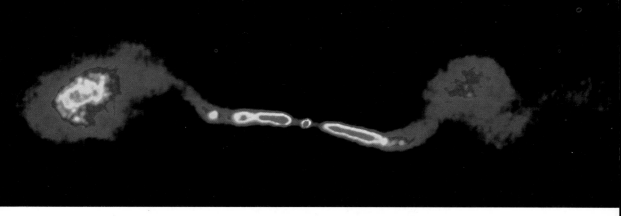

Radio telescopes can convert signals into computer images.

nearby stars on all those channels would have taken Drake and the other early hunters millions of years!

In addition, radio telescopes are used almost all of the time to study natural radio signals from stars. Little time was available for those who wanted to find alien signals with them.

CURRENT SETI PROJECTS

Interest in finding alien radio signals grew during the early 1980s. People began referring to the "search for extraterrestrial intelligence" as *SETI*. SETI was made by combining the "s" from "search," the "e" from "extra," the "t" from "terrestrial," and the "i" from "intelligence."

By 1982 Dr. Paul Horowitz, a Harvard

Dr. Paul Horowitz

physics professor, had developed a special system for finding alien signals. His system could study 128,000 separate channels at once. Dr. Horowitz's system was called Suitcase SETI because it was portable and could be attached to an available radio telescope.

In 1982 Dr. Horowitz attached Suitcase SETI to the huge radio telescope at Arecibo, Puerto Rico. For 75 hours Horowitz hunted for radio signals from 250 nearby stars. Because it could study 128,000 channels at once, Suitcase SETI listened as much in a minute as Project Ozma could have

Kitt Peak National Observatory near Tucson, Arizona

done in 100,000 years! Yet
Horowitz captured no alien
signals. This was not
surprising. He had studied
a small number of stars.
And he had not spent much
time on any of them.

By 1985 Dr. Horowitz had built a better receiver than Suitcase SETI. It is called META (for Megachannel Extra-Terrestrial Assay). META can study 8.4 million channels at once. It also has a permanent home — the 84-foot Harvard University/Smithsonian radio telescope at Harvard, Massachusetts.

Night and day, META has been hunting alien radio signals since fall of

The 84-foot radio dish at Harvard, Massachusetts

1985. Dr. Horowitz concentrates on "magic frequencies." These are ones that, because of their scientific meaning, aliens might use if they wanted to contact us. It takes about nine months for META to scan the whole

sky at a magic frequency.
After completing each
scan, Dr. Horowitz moves
on to another magic
frequency.

Each day an assistant at
the radio telescope checks
the computer to see if
META has found an alien
signal. None has yet been
found. Even if such signals
are being sent out,
locating one with META or
with several other SETI
projects in the United

Very Large Array Radio Telescopes at Socorro, New Mexico

States and Russia could take many years.

The most powerful SETI system yet is being developed by NASA (the U.S. National Aeronautics and Space Administration). Several radio telescopes

The Gamma Ray Observatory

will be used in the NASA program, which should be under way by about 1991.

The NASA project will search the sky for strong signals. About 1,000 stars similar to the Sun will be studied closely.

WHAT IF WE FIND A SIGNAL?

What if one day Dr. Horowitz or a NASA scientist captures an alien radio signal? What excitement there would be! We would know that we are not alone in the universe. And think of all we might learn from an

Artists used the writings of H. G. Wells to draw moon people (left) and Martians (right). But no one knows what intelligent life may be sending signals from other planets.

alien civilization. They might teach us how to conquer diseases and solve many other scientific mysteries.

There would be one problem with having a conversation with the aliens, though. If they were 20 light-years away, it would take 20 years between each part of the conversation!

WORDS YOU SHOULD KNOW

astronauts(AST • roh • nawts) — space explorers

astronomers(ast • RON • ih • merz) — people who study stars, planets, and other heavenly bodies

billion(BIL • yun) — a thousand million (1,000,000,000)

extraterrestrial(x • tra • ter • REST • tree • ull) — from beyond Earth

flying saucers(FLY • ing SAW • serz) — unproven objects thought by some people to be alien spacecraft

intelligent(in • TEL • ih • gent) — having a good brain

light-year(LITE YEER) — the distance that light, which moves at 186,000 miles per second, travels in a year; a light-year equals about 5.88 trillion miles

"magic frequencies"(MAJ • ik FREE • kwen • ceez) — channels which, due to their scientific importance, aliens might use if they wanted to contact us

million(MIL • yun) — a thousand thousand (1,000,000)

NASA — the National Aeronautics and Space Administration, a U.S. agency

orbit(OR • bit) — the path an object takes when moving around another object

planets(PLAN • ets) — objects that orbit stars

Project Ozma(PRAH • ject AHZ • ma) — the first search for alien radio signals (made in 1960)

Proxima Centauri(PROX • ih • ma sen • TAW • ree) — the nearest star to the Sun, 4.3 light-years away

radio telescopes(RAY • dee • oh TEL • ih • skohpz) — instruments that collect radio waves from distant objects

SETI(SET • ee) — a short way of saying "search for extraterrestrial intelligence"

Solar System(SO • ler SISS • tim) — the Sun and all objects that orbit it. Other stars may also have solar systems

speed of light(SPEED UV LITE) — about 186,000 miles per second

stars(STARZ) — giant balls of hot, glowing gas

telescopes(TEL • ih • skohpz) — instruments that make distant objects look closer

trillion(TRIL • yun) — a thousand billion (1,000,000,000,000)

unidentified flying objects(un • eye • DEN • tih • fide) (UFO's) — unknown objects in the sky

universe(YOO • nih • verse) — all of space and everything in it

INDEX

About the author

*Dennis Fradin attended Northwestern University on a partial
creative scholarship and was graduated in 1967. His previous
books include the Young People's Stories of Our States series for
Childrens Press, and Bad Luck Tony for Prentice-Hall. In the True
book series Dennis has written about astronomy, farming, comets,
archaeology, movies, space colonies, the space lab, explorers, and
pioneers. He is married and the father of three children.*